The Vegetables Group

BY ANNABELLE TOMETICH

The Child's World

Published by The Child's World®
1980 Lookout Drive • Mankato, MN 56003-1705
800-599-READ • www.childsworld.com

Acknowledgments
The Child's World®: Mary Berendes, Publishing Director
Red Line Editorial: Editorial direction
The Design Lab: Design
Amnet: Production
Photographs ©: Front cover: FoodIcons; BrandX Images; BrandX Images,
3, 4, 6, 8, 10, 12, 14, 23; choosemyplate.gov, 5; FoodIcons, 7, 20;
Elena Schweitzer/Shutterstock Images, 9; Tatyana Vychegzhanina/
Shutterstock Images, 11; Nick Osborne/Shutterstock Images, 13;
Infografick/Shutterstock Images, 15; Kids in Motion, 16; Monkey
Business Images/Shutterstock Images, 17; Shane Trotter/Shutterstock
Images, 19; Eurobanks/Shutterstock Images, 21

ISBN: 978-1623236069
LCCN: 2013931381

Printed in the United States of America
Mankato, MN
July, 2013
PA02178

ABOUT THE AUTHOR

Annabelle Tometich writes about food
and restaurants for *The News-Press*, a
newspaper and multimedia company in
Fort Myers, Florida. During her time as a
sportswriter for *The News-Press*, Annabelle
won three awards from the Associated
Press Sports Editors. She lives in Fort Myers
with her husband and young son.

Table of Contents

CHAPTER ONE

Eating Plants

Have you ever seen a cow chomping on grass in the middle of a field? That grass is a plant, like the trees in your neighborhood and the flowers in your yard. **Vegetables** such as carrots, broccoli, and corn are plants, too. You need vegetables to help you grow. Vegetables are packed with **nutrients** that help build strong bones, healthy eyes, and lean muscles.

The MyPlate diagram shows the five food groups that make up a healthy diet: protein, grains, dairy, fruits, and vegetables. The diagram shows what your plate or bowl should look like at every meal. Vegetables should cover about a quarter of

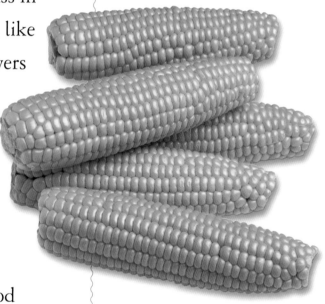

▲ Sweet corn is a tasty summertime vegetable.

▶ Opposite page: Vegetables fill one-quarter of the MyPlate plate.

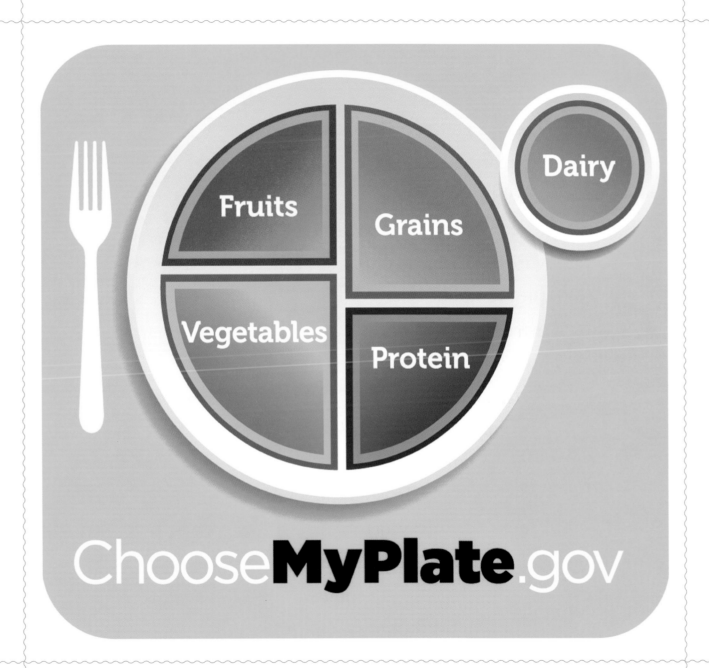

ChooseMyPlate.gov

your plate. Vegetables and fruits together should cover half of your plate.

Vegetables are any part of a plant that can be safely eaten and are usually not sweet. Most vegetables do not have seeds. Vegetables can be the root of the plant, like carrots. They can also be the stem of the plant, like celery. Some vegetables are the leaves of the plant, like spinach. Others are the flower of the plant, like broccoli.

Foods such as pumpkins, cucumbers, eggplants, and squash have seeds. Scientifically, they are fruits. However, they are commonly considered vegetables because they are not as sweet as most fruits. **Legumes**, such as lima beans and peanuts, are also vegetables. Legumes are very high in

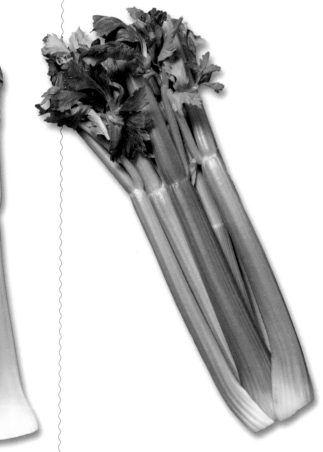

▲ Celery is vegetable that is the stalk of a plant.

protein and can take the place of meat for people on vegetarian diets.

Vegetables come in all shapes and sizes from tiny peas to giant heads of cabbage that can weigh over 100 pounds. No matter how you eat your vegetables, they are essential to a healthy diet. A healthy diet helps make a healthy you.

▶ Eat different kinds of vegetables for a balanced diet.

CHAPTER TWO

How Vegetables Build Muscles

▶ Opposite page: Nutrients in vegetables help your body grow.

▼ Carrots and other vegetables contain vitamins, minerals, and fiber.

Vegetables are full of **vitamins**, **minerals**, and **fiber**. The next time you eat a carrot stick, imagine your stomach breaking down each bite into tiny building blocks. These blocks are so small you cannot see them with a magnifying glass.

These itty-bitty building blocks are called vitamins and minerals. They enter your blood after you eat healthy foods such as vegetables. Your blood carries them throughout your body and delivers them to your brain, heart, lungs, bones, and muscles. The vitamin and mineral

building blocks help you grow and become stronger. They also help keep you from getting sick.

Vegetables are packed with different vitamins. Vitamin A is a nutrient found in carrots. It helps keep your eyes strong and your vision clear. Red peppers are full of vitamin C. Vitamin C helps wounds heal and keeps skin and joints healthy. Spinach is high in vitamin K, which helps your blood **clot** and prevents bruises from forming. Spinach is also high in iron and manganese. These minerals help you grow. They keep your bones and muscles healthy.

Vegetables are also filled with fiber. Fiber is the part of the vegetable that cannot be broken down in your stomach. Fiber keeps your heart healthy and helps you feel full longer. Fiber keeps things moving in your **digestive tract**. It helps move food from your stomach through your **intestines**. Fiber

▲ These colorful vegetables contain nutrients such as vitamin A, vitamin C, and vitamin K.

NIGHT VISION FROM CARROTS?
During World War II, fighter pilot John Cunningham became the most accomplished night pilot in the British Air Force. The air force told everyone his exceptional sight came from eating carrots. Although carrots help your eyes, they do not give you night vision. The air force made up the story to hide its use of radar. Radar was the real reason Cunningham could see so well in the dark.

helps you have healthy **bowel** movements. Good bowel movements are as important to your health as strong muscles and good vision.

By following the MyPlate diagram and covering a quarter of your plate in vegetables, you can be sure your body is getting all the building blocks it needs.

▶ Salad is a great way to add vegetables to your dinner plate.

CHAPTER THREE

Vegetables Around the World

When you walk through the **produce** department at your grocery store, you see a lot of the same vegetables. Broccoli, corn, peppers, and lettuce are common vegetables in the United States. But in other parts of the world, these vegetables can be rare. People get their nutrients from many different kinds of vegetables, including some you may have never seen.

▲ Broccoli is a common vegetable in the United States.

▶ Bok choy is a popular Asian vegetable.

Asia

In Asian countries such as China and Japan, bok choy is a popular vegetable. Bok choy is a type of cabbage that looks like a cross between celery and lettuce. Its leaves are white at the center and darker green around the edges. It is used in stir-fries and salads. It can be boiled in soups. Other popular Asian vegetables include daikon radish, seaweed, long beans, and edamame.

Africa

Yams are a popular vegetable in West African countries such as Nigeria and Ghana. Yams are very large and have white or yellow flesh. You must cook yams to eat them safely. You can boil, roast, bake, or mash yams. You can also fry them as chips. Yams can grow to be more than 4 feet long and can weigh more than 150 pounds. Other popular African vegetables include cassava, eggplant, garlic, and spinach.

South and Central America

The chayote (pronounced chiye-YO-tee) grows in Brazil, Costa Rica, and Mexico. It is a type of gourd. Chayote is closely related to melons, cucumbers, and squash. It is pear-shaped with bumpy, light-green skin. Some people say chayote tastes like a cross between cucumber and raw potato. Chayote can be boiled, baked, mashed, or fried. Other popular vegetables in South

▲ Yams are vegetables enjoyed by people in West Africa.

▶ Chayote tastes like a cucumber and raw potato put together.

and Central America include beans, tomatillo, cassava, and corn.

Europe

Leeks are a vegetable used in British, German, and Italian cuisines. Leeks are a vegetable closely related to onions and garlic. Leeks can grow as long as your arm. They are white toward the bottom and green at the top. Leeks can be sautéed, boiled, or even fried like onion rings. Other popular vegetables in Europe include olives, Brussels sprouts, Belgian endive, and artichokes.

CHAPTER FOUR

Vegging Out

Vegetables are packed with nutrients that help you grow bigger and run faster. Kids ages four to eight should eat 1 1/2 cups of vegetables every day. Girls who are nine to 13 years old should eat at least 2 cups of vegetables per day. Nine- to 13-year-old boys should eat 2 1/2 cups of vegetables per day. If you run around a lot, dance, or play sports, then you should eat even more vegetables to help power your activities. How can you reach that goal? You can buy and try more vegetables and make more vegetable dishes.

The next time you go to the grocery store, walk through the produce department with your parents

▲ Fuel your dance moves with veggies!

and take a look at all of the colorful vegetables lining the shelves. Pick out one of your favorite vegetables. Then pick out one you have never tried before or one you have not tried in a long time.

Studies have shown that the more times you taste a vegetable, the more likely you are to enjoy it. Healthy vegetables you do not like now you may enjoy later. As you grow up, your taste for vegetables grows up, too. Eating vegetables

▶ What will you pick as your favorite vegetable at the grocery store?

throughout the day makes it easy to reach your MyPlate goal. Here are some ideas on how you can add vegetables to every meal:

Breakfast: Add fresh or reheated frozen vegetables to eggs in the morning. Top grits with sautéed tomatoes or broccoli for a jolt of vitamins and fiber. Add a handful of raw spinach leaves to your fruit smoothie. The spinach will make your drink green, but you will only taste the sweetness of the fruit.

Lunch: Have fun with salads by trying new types of lettuces and greens for the base. Top them with the most colorful tomatoes, carrots, cucumbers, and other vegetables you can find. Use large romaine lettuce leaves in place of bread to make lettuce wraps. Fill them with your favorite meats and cheeses and more vegetables.

Dinner: Make super-veggie pizzas. Use a blender to **puree** carrots and peppers and other

HOW CARROTS GOT INTO CAKE
In the Middle Ages, sugar was very expensive. Bakers and cooks relied on naturally sugary plants such as carrots to sweeten desserts. Two and three hundred years ago, British cookbooks often featured recipes for carrot pudding. Legends say that George Washington ate a carrot teacake at a tavern in New York City in 1783. However, the vegetable-filled cakes were not popular in the United States until the 1970s. That is when people started baking carrot cakes as a healthy alternative to traditional desserts.

vegetables directly into your tomato sauce to pump up its nutrients. Put the sauce on whole-grain pizza crusts, and then add more of your favorite vegetable toppings and a sprinkle of cheese.

Snacks: Make vegetable art. Use carrots, tomatoes, cucumber slices, and celery sticks to make colorful flowers, houses, or people on your plate.

Dessert: Put vegetables into desserts, too. Grated carrots and zucchini make delicious additions to cakes and breads, as do canned pumpkin and boiled, mashed sweet potatoes. These vegetables keep cakes moist and make them much more nutritious.

Vegetables are delicious any time of day. Just like proteins, fruits, grains, and dairy, vegetables are a key part of the MyPlate diagram. When you eat plenty of vegetables, you are building a healthy plate and a healthy body, too.

▲ Carrot cake is a sweet treat.

Hands-on Activity: Celery Cars

These are vegetables with wheels. You can fill these veggie cars with peanut butter or cream cheese. Just be sure to eat them quickly, before they drive away!

What You'll Need:

A rib of celery cut in half, two toothpicks, four carrot coins, some raisins, and peanut butter or cream cheese

Directions:

1. First, use a butter knife to spread peanut butter or cream cheese into the cavity of the celery rib.
2. Then, with the peanut butter side facing up, poke a toothpick into the front end of the celery, pushing it all the way through until you have an equal amount of toothpick sticking out of either side.
3. Repeat with the second toothpick, pushing it through toward the back of the celery rib. The toothpicks are the car's axles. Next,

carefully push your carrot wheels onto these toothpick axles until they are firmly attached.

4. Place your raisins in the peanut butter as celery-car passengers. *Vroom, vroom*, eat up!

Glossary

bowel (BOW-uhl): Bowel is another word for your intestines, which are where digested food travels to after leaving your stomach. Your bowel is part of the digestive tract.

clot (klot): To clot is to stick together. Vitamin K helps blood clot.

digestive tract (dye-JESS-tiv trakt): The digestive tract is a series of tubes that pass food through your body after you eat it. The digestive tract breaks food down into minerals and vitamins your body can use.

fiber (FYE-ber): Fiber is the part of plant foods the body cannot break down. Fiber helps with healthy digestion.

intestines (in-TES-tinz): The intestines are long tubes in a person's body that digest food after it leaves his or her stomach. Humans have large intestines and small intestines.

legumes (LEG-yoomz): Legumes are members of a plant family with seed pods that split on both sides. Beans, peas, lentils, and peanuts are legumes.

minerals (MIN-er-ulz): Minerals are substances found in foods. Minerals such as magnesium, calcium, and iron help the body stay healthy.

nutrients (NOO-tree-entz): Nutrients are substances the body needs to grow. Vitamins and minerals are nutrients.

produce (PRO-doos): The word produce is a collective term for agricultural products, especially fruits and vegetables. The produce section in your grocery store is full of healthy vegetables.

puree (pyoo-RAY): When you puree, you blend fruits or vegetables until they are smooth and liquid-like. Puree vegetables and add them to tomato sauce.

vegetables (VEJ-tuh-bulz): Vegetables are parts of plants that can be eaten, including the leaves, stems, roots, and flowers. Beets, carrots, and potatoes are all vegetables.

vitamins (VYE-tuh-minz): Vitamins are substances found in foods that help the body stay healthy and function properly. Vitamins are found in vegetables and fruits.

To Learn More

BOOKS

Jonath, Leslie, and Ethel Brennan. *At the Farmers Market with Kids: Recipes and Projects for Little Hands.* San Francisco: Chronicle, 2012.

Mateljan, George. *The World's Healthiest Food: Essential Guide for the Healthiest Way of Eating.* Seattle, WA: GMF Publishing, 2006.

WEB SITES

Visit our Web site for links about vegetables: **childsworld.com/links**

Note to Parents, Teachers, and Librarians: We routinely verify our Web links to make sure they are safe and active sites. So encourage your readers to check them out!

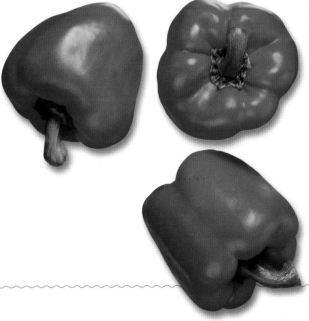

Index